T0207685

# A TEACHER'S STORYBOOK

### Lessons Learned Over Time,
### Lessons of a Different Kind

## RAYMOND J. GOLARZ
## WITH MARION SIMPSON GOLARZ

**author**HOUSE®

AuthorHouse™
1663 Liberty Drive
Bloomington, IN 47403
www.authorhouse.com
Phone: 1 (800) 839-8640

Published by AuthorHouse  12/16/2019

ISBN: 978-1-7283-3554-4 (sc)
ISBN: 978-1-7283-3553-7 (e)

Library of Congress Control Number: 2019918277

Print information available on the last page.

This book is printed on acid-free paper.

# DEDICATION

**To Our Children and Grandchildren**

# CONTENTS

# Acknowledgements

To my father "Lefty" Golarz who taught to me the love of storytelling,

To my friend Gary Phillips who taught me how to refine the telling,

To my wife Marion who helped me move the spoken story to the written one.

To our daughter Tanya Scherschel who edited the written word.

# Foreword

When man first drew pictures on the wall of a cave, he was conveying messages about his life. Often his messages seemed to contain knowledge about what he saw as critical to his survival. Of course, it is also possible he simply might have been trying to capture images of the creatures and natural environment that sustained him or captivated him. Whatever his reason, he was attempting to communicate something important or special about the essence of his life. He was our first storyteller—he was our first teacher.

As time passed, man continued to want to share his knowledge not only about the challenges facing him, his family and community, but also about what he saw that was special about his life. Because he had developed a more sophisticated language, he no longer needed to make crude drawings on the wall of a cave. The stories he could now share with his children and grandchildren were told in such a way that they could be passed from generation to generation. He too was a storyteller and a teacher.

As man became even more sophisticated, he learned how to put pen to paper. Eventually he was able to send voices and images through the ether to little boxes in people's homes. But his purpose continued to be the same as that man who drew pictures on a cave wall or the man who relayed tales most likely while sitting around a table or a campfire. These stories continued to tell the story about the challenges man faced, what his world was like, or perhaps what was simply important or special about the essence of his life.

And that is what this storyteller—this teacher—is doing with this collection of stories and several poignant essays. Some are sad, some funny. Some are discouraging, some uplifting. All of them offer insights gathered over 40 years of experience as a teacher, social worker, administrator, keynote speaker, parent, and citizen.

These true stories and the several essays have more than one purpose. They celebrate the efforts of so many dedicated teachers and other caring people who have tried to improved the lives of their fellow man. They also challenge the belief-systems that have formed our ideas about the mission of our society, the capacity and potential of each of us to learn, and the necessity to assure that adequate resources and talent are correctly provided and shared with everyone.

Above all, they are about the often unrecognized heroes who stay and work in our classrooms, administrative offices, neighborhoods and communities because they love children and want to make their lives safer, richer, and more productive so that they too can tell their own stories that will teach us about what is important, what is possible, what is true, and what is special about all our lives.

MJG

# PREFACE

My father was a storyteller. I would often sit at the kitchen table and listen for hours as he would take me to places I had never been. As I grew older, my interest in listening did not wane even though the stories were ones I had heard. It may have been his enthusiasm, possibly the way he gestured, maybe his voice—the inflections, variations in volume, or possibly it was the joy in his face and smile. Maybe it was all of those things for, you see, my father was a storyteller.

In my late 20's, I began teaching college courses in the evenings. During the day, I worked with delinquent youth and gangs in poverty communities near the South Side of Chicago. Eventually, my students included law enforcement officers, primarily from Chicago. I found very quickly that when I delivered the course content in story form, those in my classes were engaged and understood the concepts more deeply.

Over time, I came to know what stories or occasional provocative essays they enjoyed most and which ones best facilitated their learning. What I did not know was that my former students would often ask other students currently taking my class, "Has he told you the story about *Danny and Charlie* yet? You'll remember that one for a long time." I was touched. They were enjoying sitting at the kitchen table.

In the early 80's, Dr. Gary Phillips asked me to assist in the training of school communities in the inner-city of Chicago. The director of those 131 schools was Dr. Phedonia Johnson. For the next three years, I did training in each of those schools, always using the medium of stories. After that experience, I began keynoting conferences throughout the United States and Canada, eventually keynoting in every state except two and in every Province in Canada, again always using stories as the medium.

The pieces contained in this book are a potpourri. For the most part they are stories with a sprinkling of essays. Some focus upon the crushing impact of poverty, some upon the need for honor and dignity, some upon the power of belief, others about the devastating horrors of prejudice. As you read, I hope that you will listen, as I did at the kitchen table, and become mesmerized.

Finally, when you finish the book, I hope that you will turn to those reading after you and ask excitedly, "Have you gotten to the story about Danny and Charlie yet? You'll remember that one for a long time."

**RJG**

# LESSONS LEARNED

*As an educator you soon learn that if you keep your eyes and heart open you will find magnificence all around you and thus you will be consistently rewarded with unanticipated gifts.*

# Do you enjoy Chopin?

~

I T WAS A VERY COLD, windy, late November Saturday morning with traces of snow in the air as I was completing my drive to Dumas Elementary School on Chicago's South Side. The neighborhood had the look of post WWII Germany with only a sprinkling of very old houses, most abandoned—some simply in disrepair. The few business establishments had iron grates on all of their windows and doors. The occasional oil-drum fires where heavily clothed men gathered in an attempt to keep warm were the only signs of human occupancy.

I continued to drive. Slowly more houses and businesses came into view. Finally, I came upon a one story brick school building. I pulled up and turned off my car. Almost immediately four fairly good sized men approached and surrounded my car. I was anxious. The largest leaned over close to my driver side window and asked, "Are you Dr. Golarz?" I nodded. In an authoritative tone he said, "Come with us. We're your body guards." In the building, Sylvia Peters, the principal, wrapped her arms around me and said, "Thanks for coming. Welcome to Dumas."

Some months earlier I had agreed to keynote her school's Celebration of Learning. Sylvia introduced me to four of her sixth-grade students—three girls and a boy. She told me, "These children have won the honor of showing you around their school. They all led the entire school and community in the annual candle-light ceremony this year. Please go with them." I nodded and then the smallest of the three girls took my hand, looked up, smiled and said,

1

"Dr. Golarz, do you enjoy Chopin?" I was completely taken aback and then responded, "Why, yes, I do." As we walked, the young man chimed in, "Chopin is our composer of the month. All of our language arts and our creative writings have him and his music as our central theme. Last month it was Schubert and next month Handel."

As we talked, we passed by classroom after classroom. Each classroom door was decorated with a collage of pictures and historical information which related to a particular composer. I had not expected to experience what I was being shown. Is this school what our nation defines as dysfunctional? Then Sylvia explained that though the great composers' curricular design had brought immense pride to her school and community, it was but one of the strategies designed to facilitate student capacity and their more extensive depth of knowing.

She explained further that she had cajoled local businesses into donating violins, cellos, woodwinds, brass, and percussion instruments so that Dumas Elementary could have an orchestra—a meaningful connection to the composers her students were studying and a touch of class to match the new found dignity of her students and their community. Sixty years of educational research affirms that individual schools are the most effective units of improvement— never state legislatures. Dumas was an excellent example of this.

As I drove away, the neighborhood seemed a little brighter. Most of Sylvia's students were still struggling to read at grade level, most were still hungry when they woke up each morning, and most would never experience a home with both a father and a mother—many with neither parent. But they had a neighborhood public school that offered hope and provided pride.

As for me, I got a special gift that snowy, November morning, for whenever I hear the music of Chopin, I picture the beautiful, proud face of a young African-American girl who captured my heart and said to me with a smile, "Dr. Golarz, do you enjoy Chopin?"

*Unless we understand the depth of the pain of those who are our fellowmen, we will assuredly never understand them.*

# THE ADVOCATE

~

I HAD JUST FINISHED PARTICIPATING IN a case conference, the purpose of which was to rewrite an IEP (individualized educational plan) for a special needs fourth-grader in our school system. After the conference I asked Martha (the boy's mother) to join me in my office. Besides representing her son, Martha advocated for many district children. She had an in-depth understanding of special education law and a profound sensitivity for special needs children.

Resources available for special needs children have always been inadequate. From its beginning in the early 1970s, the special education mandate has never been adequately funded. Martha, besides advocating for individual children, always helped me with the legislative and funding issues. She was tireless in this regard.

We met that afternoon and plotted some legislative strategies for the coming general assembly session. As we completed our work, I asked Martha if she would mind a personal question. She nodded and said, "Go ahead, Ray." So I said, "Martha, you are a truly extraordinary advocate and you have the persistence of a junkyard dog. Can you help me understand the source of your endless zeal?" She looked at me for a long moment and then asked, "Ray, do you mind if I close the door?" I said, "No, of course not."

She then began, "If a child's special needs are not clearly identified, most of us tend to assume he is normal and treat the child accordingly. My son Timmy seemed normal. So, when Timmy transgressed we assumed that he was being defiant or stubborn. By the time he was six, dealing with him alone took ten times the effort and strength I needed to deal with our other children. Jack left for work early each morning and typically didn't get home until 6:00 p.m. By evening each day I was exhausted. If I hadn't slept the night before, I was a zombie. On one of those days I had reached my limit. I grabbed Timmy by his shoulders and then screamed at him. I said, "Get out, leave this house, go away and don't come back."

When I regained my composure I began to prepare supper. The house seemed unusually quiet. Then something told me to look for Timmy. So I did. I looked everywhere but could not find him. Panic set in, and I went outside searching the neighborhood, now screaming out his name. When Jack got home I gave him a brief explanation then took his car.

The cold rain was turning to sleet. The car was sliding as I braked on freezing streets. I was making bigger and bigger circles away from our home. I finally got to the main boulevard. Traffic was heavy. Standing on the corner was this sad and pathetic six-year-old holding a stick on his shoulder with cans of food at the end of the stick wrapped in a bathroom towel. I jumped from the car leaving it in the street and screamed "Timmy." He looked up at me and said through his tears, "I am so sorry, Mommy. I did what you said and left but I don't know where to go."

I grabbed him and hugged and held him. As I knelt there holding him, I vowed that I would never again hurt him—nor would I ever let anyone else hurt him.

A month later, we got his psychological evaluation that included a listing of the behaviors over which he most likely had no control. She said no more.

She didn't have to.

We sat silently looking out the window at the setting sun.

*Teaching with its profound impact doesn't happen every day. But when it does…..ah, when it does, how special and often lifelong that impact is. All teachers can tell you about such times, for they are the cherished, lifelong memories of teachers. Following is one such story.*

# DANNY AND CHARLIE

~

D ANNY CAME TO MY SEVENTH grade class from foster care, placed in the school district with a loving family. He could neither read nor write. He was a tall, gangly, timid boy. I did not know of his deficiencies until he handed in his first in-class writing assignment. What he handed in was a page filled with lines of scribbling, blank space, more scribbling, blank space, more scribbling, blank space, on and on, line after line. There were no words. My heart ached. It ached more as I observed him at recess preferring to play with first and second graders. His foster parents, the principal, and I met. We did not conclude with a viable plan to help Danny—merely a commitment to find one.

Several days later on a rainy fall morning when the "walkers" were permitted early entry into the school building, I observed Danny sitting on a stair with a classmate, Charlie. Charlie was short and overweight, extremely shy and very bright. Yet as shy as Charlie was and as timid as Danny was, they appeared to be enjoying their conversation and moment of camaraderie. I had been praying for an opportunity and here it was so I took it and ran.

After school that same day, knowing that they were both "walkers," I asked them to assist me in taking equipment to the park (football practice field) three blocks away. They talked all the way to the park, completely ignoring my presence.

A second writing assignment came. I advised Danny that he did not need to do it. He looked up at me and said, "Coach, if I can find a way to do it, will you take it?" I said, "Sure, Danny, sure." The day the assignment was due, Charlie and Danny came to me. Charlie turned in his assignment and then the two of them handed me another paper. Charlie explained, "For a week Danny has been making up this story and memorizing it. Yesterday I wrote it for him. He knows he can't write yet. But, it is his story. Will you take it?" I kept that paper for many years. The story was very elegant in its simplicity.

I knew Charlie wanted to do something athletic. So I would occasionally give the two of them a basketball and let them go out on the playground's far end for twenty minutes or so to practice. Eventually, they would come to me after school to get the basketball and play until dark.

A treasured memory I still have is looking out of my third floor classroom window and watching the two of them, arm over arm, walking home, a vision that always brings a smile to my face.

Charlie got pretty good at basketball. He was hard to beat at the game of horse. Danny, mostly with Charlie's help, learned to write. Their friendship was lifelong.

*Veteran teachers have learned to be prepared for just about anything. Tragically there are some things that defy preparation.*

# A TEACHER'S WORST NIGHTMARE

~

MY PHONE RANG. IT WAS a teacher colleague from California.
"Ray?"

"Yeah, Dan."

"You watchin' CNN?"

"No, out having lunch."

"Watch CNN. Our school's on lock-down. I can see two, no, three helicopters. At the entrance way of the building there are police in helmets separating hundreds of black and Hispanic students—fights all over campus. God, hope they can get this under control. DAMN. Shot just fired through a window of my classroom.

EVERYBODY ON THE FLOOR NOW, NOW! Ray, can't talk."

Terror enveloped my soul for Dan followed immediately by a rush of memories that took me back in time.

The phone was ringing and my secretary Phyllis was screaming to me.

"It's Chief Wise—Police Department."

"George?"

"Ray, we have a full-blown situation erupting on the streets surrounding Central High. We're alerting your school staff, but this thing looks like it will overrun our resources. We'll be calling upon the East Chicago and Chicago police for help. You might want to delay dismissal in some of your surrounding schools until we get this under control."

I hung up, crossed the office area and went directly into the superintendent's office. "John, just talked to Chief Wise. Here's the situation." I explained and then we divided the emergency assignments. Soon we had informed all personnel who needed to know, put into place emergency procedures, and had updated news services. At that point central high school called and advised us that some involved in the rioting had entered the north end of their building. Young adults carrying arms were seen.

With a fellow administrator who had done extensive work with the rioting communities, I drove to the scene. We could see men standing on corners holding hand guns and carrying rifles and shotguns. Many we did not know. They appeared to be older. They were drinking heavily and throwing bottles at passing cars.

We got out of my car near the football field. It was at that moment that I was most terrified, for coming out of a neighborhood of mostly southern whites were seven or eight men. They were carrying weapons of all kinds including shot guns and hand guns. They were moving toward the high school. My terror was knowing that if they walked far enough without changing direction, the corner of the high school building that was obstructing their view would no longer block their sight-line and they would be able to see the armed group of black American men on Calumet Avenue.

At that moment two police squad cars, siren and lights on, came careening at breakneck speed around the corner from Sohl Street moving directly toward them. The gang of whites fired several of their weapons and then scattered quickly into the neighborhood. For the next four hours the police slowly yet steadily were regaining control of the neighborhoods and streets.

Somewhere near 7:30 p.m., faculty and staff were beginning to gather in the high school cafeteria. Many were in shock. Some had vomited. Others would soon do so. Others were sitting and shaking, while still others just stared blindly into space. Some teachers who had assumed leadership were moving from teacher to teacher, trying to calm frayed nerves or just hold those who could not stop shaking. They would continue tending to their comrades until all were safely out of the building. The next day there would be no schooling, nor the day afterwards, nor the week after that. It takes time to bandage psychological bleeding.

My thoughts retuned to my friend Dan, and then I said a prayer for teachers everywhere.

*As I traveled our country keynoting conferences, I found often that I came away with more than I gave. Once, in North Carolina, I was given the gift of this following story.*

# MIKE THE BUS DRIVER

~

H IS NAME WAS MIKE. HE was a school bus driver. His assignment was bussing children in grades one through four. He liked his work—he liked kids. Earlier in life he had been a fighter pilot. A war injury ended his service, but Mike had no regrets. Driving a bus and daily seeing young faces was a good life.

One day a senior administrator asked him to deliver a note to the building librarian. Mike accidently entered an auditorium where a faculty meeting was in progress. Leaving would have created a disruption, so he sat down quietly. He intended to leave as soon as he could. While waiting, he heard the principal express a deep concern. "My colleagues, many of our students seem not to appreciate their good work. I know you are aware of this, for you have told me so. I have no immediate answer, so I ask you to assist me in any way you can with some resolution."

The meeting ended and Mike quietly left. Though simply a bus driver, he thought possibly he might help. He had noted for quite some time how his students often left their graded school work on the bus. It had saddened him particularly to see so many of the papers with stars and smiley faces strewn across the floor. He knew, of course, why they left them, for he knew his route. Most of his students went home to empty houses so there was no one to show these papers to.

Mike decided to do what he thought could be his part. He announced to all of the students riding his bus that he wanted to see their good work—especially the work with the stars and smiley faces. When they did this, he expressed appropriate compliments to them for such work. Then he would sign "Mike" in the upper- right-hand corner of their paper with what he called his "Magic Christmas red pen." Soon Mike found that at the end of his evening run, the bus was much less littered. There were never again papers on the floor bearing stars and or smiley faces. Teachers began to notice that children were requesting more of these rewards and showing an increased willingness to work for them. It didn't take teachers long to find the source of enthusiasm. It did take a little longer for Mike to load his late afternoon bus run, but everyone seemed willing to work around that.

Eventually, Mike passed away. The number of young children and parents who came to his funeral was moving. Shortly after his death, an unexpected practice began to occur. Graffiti began to show up on the outside of the bus Mike drove, always a star or smiley face and always in red. Authorities never looked for the perpetrators, nor were the drawings ever washed or wiped off. Eventually, over time, they simply faded away.

My story-teller then told me her name and advised me that she was now a teacher at that same school. Without saying anything else, she very carefully pulled from her purse an old, yet neatly folded paper—her own personal work product from so many years ago. On the paper were a star, a smiley face, and the name "Mike" written in the upper right-hand corner—a name written I'm sure with a "Magic Christmas red pen." She looked up at me and smiled. I nodded my head and smiled back.

It isn't just teachers who make magnificent differences or touch the hearts of us all.

*Some teachers are artists who can masterfully open the treasure box of profound learning. Such was Mr. Nelson. He taught poetry and literature. The poem he selected that first week of class was "Thanatopsis."*

# THE TREASURE BOX

I RECALL VIVIDLY HOW ON THAT first day Mr. Nelson enthusiastically passed out printed sheets of the poem while he danced between the aisles of our classroom chairs. This he did while simultaneously sharing in his mellow, baritone voice, stanza after stanza of Bryant's brilliant poetic gift. With each reading he seemed to go deeper and deeper into the poem. It was as if the poem and he were now in a conversation. As we students looked at each other, it was clear that we had each felt the magic he was creating. He took us far that day. He had opened that treasure box and invited us to glimpse inside. We had, however, no idea of the depth of the trip he was planning for us.

A week later he took us further—much further. Mr. Nelson had us carefully ponder, discuss, and analyze the poem. He guided us into an open conversation of mortality. Finally, cognitively exhausted, we understood Bryant—or so we thought. But Mr. Nelson wasn't finished. He looked at us and said, "My young friends, I have but one final question."

We eagerly waited, confident and cognitively ready. Then he said, "What would you do if your mother died?" I recall it seemed a strange question and for a moment he caught us off guard, but we regrouped quickly, hands going up. Responses came from all corners of the room: "I'd call other members of my family. They would need to know." "I'd search for insurance papers—we'd need those." "An obituary would be essential and there wouldn't be much time to write one."

As we were giving our answers, Mr. Nelson was moving slowly to the right-front-seat in our classroom, a seat occupied by Tony. Tony seldom said much. We all knew he was kind of slow, but no one ever laughed at him. We saw him as just a big, not-very-bright, nice kid. We had finished our responses when Mr. Nelson arrived at Tony's chair. I remember that he looked directly into Tony's face and in a quiet, gentle voice, he asked, "Tony, what would you do if your mother died?"

Tony quietly responded, "I'd cry." Mr. Nelson looked up at all of us as the room fell silent. The lid of the Treasure Box had been opened wide by a "not-very-bright" kid named Tony and an artist named Mr. Nelson who, in the silence of that classroom, watched as we all now peered in. He then said, "Bryant meant not for you to intellectually ponder death. Rather, he meant for you to feel." The journey into the poem was not meant to be a cognitive journey—rather a journey to be felt—a conversation not of minds, but of hearts.

We left class richer that day, less confident, but overwhelmed by the wisdom that could be found in the Tonys of the world. Somehow, in that brief moment in that classroom, an artist named Mr. Nelson showed us where to find our real humanity, and he did it through the magic of poetry and by pointing out for us the incredible beauty and wisdom existing within what appeared to be the simplest of our fellow man.

I don't really remember what else he taught us that year. I suppose those were the things on the standardized tests.

*I taught middle and high school. Many of my students were poor, neglected, or abused. So when an opportunity became available to direct an inner-city poverty intervention project, I accepted. Soon, as when I taught, I was learning more about poverty, abuse, neglect and delinquency than I cared to know. The intensity of my work peaked one snowy, cold, late Friday afternoon in mid- December.*

# ENDLESS SHADES OF GRAY

~

I WAS CHECKING ON A REFERRAL from the court system. The referral took me to an apartment in an old mansion built in 1880 that we called "the maze." The mansion had been cut up into no-less-than twenty small apartments. Rickety staircases lined the outside of the house, and from a distance the entire structure had the look of braided hair. I found 22B. The door was ajar.

I knocked. It opened into a gray, dark, empty room. Near the back wall was a child about four months old. He was just lying there. His breathing seemed labored. He was wet, shivering, and wearing nothing more than a very soiled diaper. I yelled but no one responded. I knocked on other apartment doors. No response. I wrapped the child in my coat and left a note, "Have your baby. Come to the Police Department."

All the way to the Police Department I couldn't get the picture of the apartment out of my mind—no toys, furniture, pictures, nor light, just endless shades of gray. I thought of my own children's bedroom—so different.

I put my hand on the child laying next to me, a child trying to breathe between deep coughs. At the station, Sgt. Wleklinski met me. He took one look at the baby and then asked, "You know Chicago Police that can get us into South Chicago Hospital's pediatric emergency center?" I responded, "Yes." "Then do it."

All the way over to the Skyway through the rapid flashing red and blue lights of the squad car, all I could envision as I held the child were those shades of gray. Poverty creates some indelible images.

The next morning about 7:00 a.m. Wleklinski called me at home. With a trembling voice, he told me that the hospital had just called and despite their best efforts, the little guy didn't make it. He was dehydrated too long. There was too much pneumonia, too much fever, just too much of everything. I thanked him for calling and hung up. I walked to the open doorway of my own children's bedroom. They were all still asleep.

As I stood there watching them with my head leaning against the door frame, a tear ran down my cheek and then several more. I didn't want to cry, but it wasn't going to be something I would decide. There are times when it happens that way. Inside of you, it just hurts.

Later I went back to classroom teaching. I never again experienced such a loss, but I and my fellow teachers were always aware of the many other children in need, like the little girl held affectionately by her kindergarten teacher because she knew that the child lived nightly with physical and sexual abuse, or the kid whose high school teacher always saved him half of her lunch because she knew it would be his only supper, or the really poor kids we all slipped a little money to so "for once" they could have the dignity of buying mom a Christmas gift.

So this Christmas season I pray, "God bless, protect, and cherish those who teach and give them needed peace."

As for the little guy, I'm sure God found for him a place of perpetual and everlasting light.

*There really is no possible way to adequately pay building principals and teachers for the work that they do. For you see, all of what they do may never be known, that is, of course, unless you come to know about it accidently.*

# THE PARENT CENTER

I T WAS A SPECTACULAR SPRING day. Over the previous two weeks we had gotten more than our fair share of mid-America rain, so the grass that had been waiting all winter was growing, touched everywhere by spring flowers. As I looked out of my office door that morning, I could see Johnny, the Director of Buildings and Grounds, walking briskly through the sun-filled hallway.

"Johnny, found that portable classroom yet?"

I was having a little fun with him. We had twelve portable one-room classrooms that we moved around to different locations in the school district as enrollments shifted and we found a need for additional space. Last year we had been using ten of the portables. Two were sitting idle. Well, one was sitting idle. The whereabouts of the second was unknown.

In the school business you get used to having some things occasionally disappear: library books, a computer, cables needed for electronic equipment, a basketball, baseball equipment, even once a fairly sizable, portable soccer backstop—but a portable classroom? Never lost a portable classroom.

I knew it was a sensitive spot for Johnny, so I let up, laughed and said, "Johnny, don't worry. We'll find it. I mean, really. How far can you get with a hot portable? Where would you fence it?" I laughed again. Johnny just looked up and shook his head.

A week or so later, Johnny and I were visiting some of our elementary schools in the central city. We were trying to get into as many classrooms as we could. Teachers never get enough visitors. When they do, they never tire of having their pupils show off regarding something that they had just learned. As superintendent, I always found it to be an uplifting experience. We left the last school on our list of morning visits, got into our car, and as we drove around the school grounds, we marveled at the manicured lawn and beautiful flower beds. The flowers surrounding the new parent center behind the school were particularly well-tended. The new parent center— what an attractive, wonderful, welcome gift to the poor parents of this community.

We stopped on the street for a moment of admiration. As we sat there, not looking at one another, Johnny asked, "Ray, what would you estimate the size of that freshly painted, one-room parent center, surrounded by beautiful flowers to be?"

"You mean is it possible that the parent center with the flower boxes under the windows and new white gutters and down spouts is about the same size as a missing classroom portable?"

We parked the car and went into the building to find Nancy the principal. On the way to her office we ran into her. "Oh, I'm so glad you're here. Have you time to stop at the parent center?"

"Nancy, that's what we need to talk to you about? Can we go to your office?"

"Sure, or we can talk at the parent center. It's not as full now as it is in the morning. Can't even find elbow room in there in the mornings."

"Full? What are you talking about, Nancy?"

"Well, we opened the center about six weeks ago. Within a week, by 6:30 a.m. it was full of young mothers. They found out that a number of our teachers were coming in early to teach a few mothers how to read. Well, they all wanted to learn to read. Run three morning classes now, an hour each, starting at 5 a.m., about twenty in a class. Teachers rotate the teaching of the classes."

"They come at 5 a.m.?"

"Some would come earlier if we were open. If they stay at home, their drunken exes or boyfriends coming in from the bars look to have their way with them, raping them if they don't consent. It's a bad situation in this neighborhood for these young women and their kids. Bad, Ray—really bad. Poor is not a good thing to be in America. But, I'm so sorry. Here I am running off at the mouth, and you wanted to talk to me about something."

I looked at Johnny, then turned to her and said, "It can wait, Nancy. It can wait."

We had our visit at the new parent center, even enjoyed doughnuts made by a few of the teachers. As we passed by the center in our car, we stopped for a final look.

"What do you think, Johnny?" Johnny quietly responded, "Think the portable we're lookin' for is smaller. Matter of fact, I'm sure it's smaller." I looked at Johnny, smiled, winked, nodded my head slowly and responded, "Think you're right, Johnny. Think you're right."

*In the movie Ben Hur, Drusus, aide to Messala, accompanies the jailer to the cell of Ben Hur's mother and sister. He inquires at the iron cell door, "If you never go into their cell, how is it you know they're still alive?" The jailor replies, "The food disappears."*

# THE FOOD DISAPPEARS

~

W HEN I BECAME SUPERINTENDENT OF schools I was sought after, invited to important community meetings, asked to speak, and complimented on my new ideas for change. At one of the grand meetings held for me, I met a woman who was introduced to me as one of our high school teachers. I recall asking her how she liked my new ideas for the district. She replied, "Forgive me. You are my fifth superintendent. If you really want my opinion, visit my classroom." Several weeks later I did.

I found to my surprise that over the past 20 years she had created in her classroom one of the most exciting remedial reading labs I had ever seen outside of fine universities. She had done it all with her own money. Most tragically, I found that I was the only administrator besides her principal to visit her classroom in those 20 years. I asked her to take part with me in next month's radio program that highlighted special school programs. She agreed on the condition that she could bring some of her students. Not only was the program done by her and her students captivating and extremely professional, more importantly, it also affirmed her worth and dignity.

The following week I visited many classrooms. Everywhere I went I found enthusiastic and exciting teaching. I was so impressed that I began to write simple short thank you notes acknowledging the moving and dedicated things I had seen. A week or so later a second grade teacher came to my office. She said through her tears, "You sent me a note. I've been teaching for 23 years and no one has ever sent me

27

a note like that before. I have it framed and it hangs behind my desk for all of my children to see. We sat late in my office that afternoon and talked of stars and smiley faces.

The author Peter Drucker asks us to consider the following questions when judging any organization's potential for greatness. I paraphrase: "Do those who work there feel treated with respect and dignity and can they take pride in knowing that someone noticed with admiration what they did?"

Through these teachers I began to understand that my new ideas were not the great ideas. I saw that my true significance and the true significance of all of the organizational leaders would be found in our capacity to honor and recognize all of those who quietly worked daily with little reward or recognition. The organization's potential for greatness was in our hands—not because of the initiation of new programs or technologies created at the top of our bureaucracies, but because we knew and could articulately speak of the work already being done by our teachers.

To be a truly great school district, our commitment to and support of those who daily serve must go far beyond our knowing simply that "the food disappears."

*A sad reality of our society is the existence of networks. They are responsible for perpetuating an uneven playing field. Further, their effect is cumulative. None of us want to acknowledge their impact, for then we must acknowledge that our success wasn't all our own doing. Great schools are essential to the success of all citizens they serve, but a level playing field might be more so.*

# Networks and the Short Form

~

I WAS LOOKING FOR A SUMMER job. My dad, a steelworker, said to me, "Go to the steel mill employment office and ask for Mr. Borbley." I went. They gave me a short form to fill out. When I got home my dad asked, "Did you see Mr. Borbley?" I said, "No, sir—just filled out the form." He sent me back. This second time I asked to see Mr. Borbley. I was then given a four-page form. While I was filling it out, an African American kid came in and was given the short form. We both finished about the same time. We turned in our forms. I was told to go back and sit down. The African American kid left. Within a few minutes, Mr. Borbley came out. We went to his office and talked, for the most part, about my dad.

The following Monday I reported to my dad's plant. The first helper who was in charge of the furnace handed me a steelworker's shovel and pointed to a large pile of manganese. I was to fill the wheelbarrow with the manganese and then, load after load, take the manganese to the side of the furnace. The temperature hovered around 130 degrees. The light wind coming off of Lake Michigan past the furnace made breathing an experience akin to exercising in a sauna. I lasted 35 minutes before dropping to my knees. I would work three months in that hellish existence. By August I had earned enough to return to college.

For years I and those like me never really acknowledged the gifts given to us by those who came before us. Rather, we suffered the illusion of our own greatness and praised one another for our youthful work ethic and persistence. In pubs over pints we would share the stories of our extraordinary worth, hard work, and heroics. Eventually, we would graduate and then with each other's assistance we would secure jobs. We would become "Mr. Borbley" to one another and eventually to our children. In due course, we would foster in our children their capacity to feel the personal exaggerated pride in themselves for their work ethic, their strength, and their entitlements.

Don't misunderstand. I am not suggesting that we and our children didn't work hard. Rather, I am suggesting that we seldom acknowledged the networks that supported us or the networks that we were creating. We would go on to forge paths for our children and create with others of our kind "networks." We would even guide our children to certain colleges because of their highly regarded networks.

The strength of networks would be as important, if not more so, than the curriculum offered. We would see no immorality in the fact that such networks were exclusionary. We would see ourselves and our children as simply talented and deserving of the benefits created by these networks. The countless unempowered kids continuing to fill out the short forms in employment offices across the country were none of our concern.

Years later I became an assistant superintendent in a large school district with five high schools and 23,000 students. One of my duties was to work with dropouts. We were losing some 500 per year to the streets and lifetimes of unemployment and shame. Many of these dropouts were capable and a few even gifted, but they were the children of the young men and women of the past generations who had received the short forms in the employment office. They had no knowledge of networks. They had no one to "speak for them."

Thus, they became vulnerable to the film-flam man who comes dressed in political garb every four years and lies to them about false enemies like immigrants. They would not be told about networks and of how things really work. They would, therefore, in their simple innocence give again to the charlatan their sacred American vote. And for this they would receive again, without their really knowing, nothing more than the short form.

*Except for Native Americans we are a nation of immigrants. We bring from our various foreign countries our dreams and our willingness to work. Do not fear us for we are you. Simply give us enough room to stand and in one generation we will strengthen the whole.*

# WHERE DREAMS CAN COME TRUE

H IS NAME WAS JOSEPH. HE was just 14 when he left his home in the village of Zagorz, located in a part of Poland known as Galicia. Over many centuries and at various times, the boundaries of this section of Poland had shifted as neighboring countries alternately claimed that this land belonged to them. Thus, the authentic citizenship of the people who were born and lived in this region was often unclear. Some people claimed their heritage to be Russian, others to be Austrian. Still others claimed to be Polish. Joseph considered himself to be Polish.

When Joseph left his home, he had with him only one change of clothing and a book of Polish hymns given to him by his father. He joined the millions of other Polish immigrants who were leaving their homeland to go to America. Like immigrants who came from countries all over the world, they were looking to escape poverty, oppression, foreign domination, and the ever-present threat of war. Their dream was to provide a better life for themselves and their families.

Once here, Joseph would meet Mary Kot, also a Polish immigrant. They would marry and eventually have five children. Joseph was full of hope that he and his family would become educated, economically secure, and able to participate in this democracy as full-fledged citizens. He was more than willing to work very hard to fulfill these dreams. He had no idea, however, just how hard life could become in this country.

Over the next 20 years he would face profound hardships. While he labored in the steel mills, he and his family lived in company housing. These accommodations were limited to one room with a single light hanging from the ceiling. Joseph and Mary hung a sheet to separate the sleeping area from the living area. Furniture was at a minimum. Barely able to provide food for his family, Joseph marched in the 1919 national steel strike where he was fired upon by his own local police. While he was not injured, friends were killed, and he assisted in their burial. As difficult as all of this was, he persisted in his efforts to make America his home.

In 1930, his second son John, an eighth-grade student at St. Mary's school, was awarded a trophy in honor of his academic achievement. Joseph was pleased. One of the reasons for his coming to America was being fulfilled. However, great difficulties still lay ahead, for in 1932 as a consequence of the Great Depression, he would be laid off and lose the house that he had built with the help of his friends. In 1935, at the height of the depression, his youngest son Andrew was suffering from diet deficiencies and had become so weak he needed special medical attention.

Only through the assistance of the General Relief Agency would Joseph's family be given the $13.00 needed to pay for such medical attention. Assistance from that General Relief Agency would later provide food. These interventions were life-saving.

For a while, things got easier. But then the United States entered into the war that was raging in Europe. In 1942, Andrew, the son who needed medical care as a child, enlisted in the United States Army along with other young Americans, many of whom were also the children of immigrants. On June 6, 1944, he and his comrades participated in the assault on Omaha Beach in Normandy. Andrew would be among the soldiers who were fortunate enough to survive. At war's end he would come home, marry, and become godfather to his brother's eldest son. He became a policeman and rose to the rank of captain in the same police department whose members had, in 1919, fired upon and killed fleeing steelworkers.

Andrew's godson—this book's author—would eventually find

his way to Indiana University where he secured his post-graduate degrees. Early in his career as an administrator, he was appointed to the position of Executive Director of the General Referral Agency of the Hammond Public Schools where for many years he would oversee the dispensing of monies to the poor—the same General Relief Agency that had given the life-saving assistance to his godfather Andrew in 1935.

Another of Joseph's grandsons would become the executive administrator responsible for employee-labor relations in that same plant where police and hired men shot and killed so many immigrant workers in the 1919 carnage. As Joseph had dreamed, his family was participating in the opportunities and challenges citizenship presented.

Joseph did not live long enough to see the continuing success and contributions his descendants achieved. One of his great granddaughters performed at Lincoln Center and another became an accomplished writer. He did not live to see one of his great grandsons play in the Rose bowl, nor another go to Africa to teach mathematics to the children of the poor, nor another receive the Bronze Star for performing surgery under fire as an American doctor in Iraq, nor another rise to the position of senior vice-president of a prestigious American firm.

Immigrants and their descendants have forever been a significant part of the cement that binds this great nation together. Joseph's story is only one of the millions of stories that tell the truth about the bright, productive, and very brave souls who have come to us from countries across this world. They have not been the burden on our schools and other institutions as some would have us believe.

On the contrary, they have risen to the levels of extraordinary success as teachers, students, soldiers, doctors, artists, and talented workers in all walks of life. With determination and sacrifice, they have earned and honored their citizenship.

Without them we would be less than the great people that we are.

*In a Christmas Carol by Charles Dickens the image of two children are shown to Scrooge. The spirit reveals to Scrooge, "This boy is ignorance, this girl want. Beware them both but most of all beware this boy for on his brow I see that written which is doom, unless the writing is erased."*

# CITIZEN'S DRUM

~

D URING MY MILITARY SERVICE I had an instructor whose daily
end-of-class challenge still resounds: "What will you read today
to help you remain an informed citizen of this American democracy.
How will you hear, as clearly as you can, the sound of the citizen's
drum?" In my youth I did not understand the depth of his meaning.
But his passionate delivery provoked a continual, lifelong reflection.
Lately I pondered. When had I first heard the sound of the citizen's
drum? And who beat that drum for me?

My reflections took me back to WWII when I sat on a kitchen
chair with my child's feet dangling as I watched my immigrant
grandmother reading her treasured newspapers. In her broken
English she would read to me of things I did not understand. What I
did understand was her love of those newspapers, the likes of which
were prohibited in her native country. Though her English was
imperfect, her reading was intense and reflected a passion to know.
She provided for me my first encounter with the sound of the citizen's
drum. I was learning of the power and the need to be informed.

As a high school student I took composition. One assignment I
was given was to write a paper that developed an argument. Several
days after turning it in, Miss Virden pulled me aside. She said, "This
is a nice start. Now find authoritative sources that challenge your
position. It is easy to create a position if you have not read and thus
not heard the argument of those who disagree." My internship in
citizenship was continuing. I was being taught to listen to the various

sounds of the drum. In college the beat continued. Careful writing of anything serious was simply expected as was the inclusion of significant related research.

For most of the twentieth century we were either at war or poised and ready to defend our way of life—democracy. Many to this end gave their lives. Others returned home forever wounded. Today, whether we are a democracy, autocracy, or dictatorship has become for many people no more than a subject for academic discourse. Many of our fellow Americans have become complacent and ignorant.

Multiple sources report that merely a third of our citizens sees democracy as essential and preferred. Only half of those graduating college will ever again in their lifetime read a book, and only half of those will read to be informed. In a national election less than 60% are likely to take the time to vote. Many fellow Americans have, through such complacency, become the "Eloi" of H.G. Well's *Time Machine*, thus increasing their vulnerability to the "Morlocks" of today.

David Brooks in a recent *New York Times* OP-ED paints an even darker picture. "At the dawn of the internet, people hoped free communication would lead to an epoch of peace, understanding and democratic communication. Instead, we're seeing polarization, alternative information universes and the rise of autocracy."

Like those of my vintage, mornings I pour my coffee and spread out local and New York papers with my wife. Most times we surf a muted TV, moving from news service to news service. Evenings we often sit with various informative magazines and books and enjoy discussions provoked by such. I have heard the sound of the drum too long to ignore it now. Like my immigrant grandmother, the quest to remain informed has become too important.

Years ago I taught government. If I were teaching today, I would attempt to convince this new generation of their obligation to become meaningfully knowledgeable—to treasure the sound of the citizen's drum. Remaining ignorant cannot be a choice. Ignorance will, in time, inevitably snatch from these citizens their irreplaceable inheritance—democracy itself.

*With my master's degree in hand from Indiana University I got a job. I had already taught middle and high school for several years, so I was a perfect fit for the school district's new, federally-funded delinquency prevention effort. They wanted staff that had some teaching experience. I thought I was prepared. I was soon to understand how much I yet had to learn.*

# THE REAL WORLD

~

MY FIRST DAY ON THE job at 7:45 a.m., I met my mentor at a house in a heavily industrialized part of town. The house was one of the few remaining in an area of condemned houses being razed as a part of a redevelopment effort. I pulled up, and Andy Hiduke was already there waiting for me.

"Have a hard time finding it, kid?"

"No, not really. Just didn't realize there were still homes in this area."

"Won't be for long, kid. Won't be for long."

I followed him up the broken concrete sidewalk to the house. Andy was an old salt—reminded me of some Navy petty officers I had served under, the kind of guys you could work with for thirty years and still not tap all that they knew or could teach you. He had been doing police and court work for years during which time he had been Chief Probation Officer for the Lake County Juvenile Court. He was a crusty, tough veteran who clearly knew his way around the darker parts of the community.

As we cautiously continued down the dangerously cracked and broken sidewalk to the house, Andy turned to me and said, "These are poor but proud people, Ray. This mother will, in her way, have cleaned the house for our coming, but it smells so bad in there that you won't notice her efforts. She may also have gotten a little coffee from somewhere and made some for us. If she offers, accept. She has little else.

Their last name is White. They have 14 children. Nine still live in the house. The two eldest sons are doing time at the state penitentiary for armed robbery. The whereabouts of two older girls and another, older son, all dropouts, are unknown." As we approached the front door, it was opened to us by a barefoot and scantily dressed boy who appeared to be about four years old.

"Hello, Mr. Andy."

Andy replied, "Joshua."

Then we heard from within the house, "Mr. Andy, you just come in here and bring your friend too."

We walked through the living room and into the kitchen. There we found Mrs. White. She was an extremely large woman. I knew from earlier conversations with Andy that she was in her mid-forties, but she appeared much older. Life had been hard. "Would you want some coffee?" We accepted and sat. One of the several young girls near the kitchen served us. Andy then advised Mrs. White that I would be working with her and her family. At this she seemed quite distressed.

She turned to me and asked, "Will you remember to bring us a food order if we need one?"

I smile and replied, "Yes, ma'am. I'll remember. I promise."

She returned my smile and seemed to relax. As Andy took over the conversation, out of the corner of my eye I watched a large roach working its way along the kitchen door frame toward a fairly sizable hole in the ceiling. While I continued to glance around from where I sat between the kitchen and living room, I could see in the living room stacks and stacks of disorganized clothing, blankets, bedding, badly-torn furniture, and mattresses. In and amongst these stacks and piles were small half-naked children playing everywhere.

I turned back to the table at the very moment that a large roach dropped from the hole in the ceiling. It landed no more than an inch from Andy's hand that was gripping his coffee mug. He did not move. He didn't in any way act startled. He did nothing to shame or humiliate this poor woman who, though she had little, was attempting to give us her best. He was the most gracious of guests.

As we left the White's house that day and went to our cars, I looked up and said a quiet "thank you." I had come to this job with my new university degree, but I had been taught more on my first day, in an old run-down house, by a seasoned mentor than I ever could have imagined. Andy looked back as he entered his car and with just a trace of a smile on his face, he slowly nodded and with a knowing look said, "Welcome to the real world, kid. Welcome to the real world."

*There are so many times that we speak and don't understand the significance of what we say. We don't understand how important, how meaningful or how necessary the words were. Maybe we really can't. So possibly we need to speak and then quietly, ever so quietly, simply be there and then hope that our presence might, for a moment, relieve the pain.*

# CAREGIVERS IN NEED OF CARE

~

I HAD BEEN INVITED TO KEYNOTE a conference in Phoenix. The day before my address, a fellow superintendent invited me to visit some elementary schools. As we walked through one of the school hallways, we noticed farther down the hall a young teacher on one knee with two second grade boys. We could see that she was attempting to resolve a fight. Tears streamed down the face of one boy. The other still had his fists clenched and a scowl on his face. As we neared, she looked up and said, "I'm so sorry, I'll get them back into class soon." I responded, "You need not apologize. We'll get out of your way."

The next morning I gave my address. Afterwards, several participants approached forming a line. Near the back of the line was the teacher who had been working the day before in the hallway with the young boys. When she finally reached me, she said, "Dr. Golarz, may I please talk to you?"

We found a quiet spot outside near a fountain and some very lovely orange trees. She began, "Today in your presentation you said that besides caring for our students, we must also remember to take care of ourselves, the caregivers. I knew when you said this that I needed to talk to you. Yesterday in the hallway at my school, I knew I should have been in my classroom teaching, but they were fighting and I had to …I had to…" She began to get choked up and was momentarily unable to continue.

I said to her, "Don't ever apologize for the work that you do.

44

Your job always includes assisting children to understand civility. You were doing the right thing." Then she blurted out, "But Dr. Golarz, it happens all the time—all the time! I have thirty-five students in my classroom, seven of whom I cannot control. I've had lots of administrative help, and I've tried all the new instructional strategies."

She went on to say, "Several veteran teachers have confided in me that no one has ever been able to handle this group. They've told me to just try to make it through the school year. But I don't know if I can. Last Tuesday, I was physically attacked and struck. An older teacher heard the noise and rushed to my aid. It's only October, just October. I can't sleep. I'm losing weight, and I'm jittery all the time. On Friday, the principal and I had a conference with a parent who yelled and screamed at me the whole time. She told me I was picking on her son, and that there were other children just as bad, and that I was racist.

"Dr. Golarz, I'm from Iowa. It was my idea to go into teaching. My dad only agreed to my teaching if I kept my other major in business. Therefore, I graduated with a double major and a 3.7 GPA. At night if I call my parents, I can hear my dad hollering in the background. He says that if things don't change soon, he's coming out on a plane, gonna punch some people out and take me home. Dr. Golarz, I so wanted to teach. It has been my dream since childhood."

She took a deep breath, dropped her head, then turned and slowly walked away. She didn't go far, just nearer the fountain in the center of the courtyard garden. I didn't follow. She needed a moment alone.

The orange trees in the courtyard didn't look quite so lovely any more.

*I am of an age where I find it entertaining to read through the ever-increasing number of ideas suggesting how to create great schools. Some, like paying teachers more than simply a living wage, or reducing class sizes have merit. Seldom, however, do we get to ideas that are transformative, but we should try.*

# Joe Went to Alaska

~

B ILL, THE PRESIDENT OF THE teachers association, came to my
office. "Ray, I have a request." He then continued. "You know Joe
Nelson—biology teacher at Central high school?" "Vaguely," I said.
"Well, Joe and I go way back, actually started teaching together some
38 years ago. He was some crackerjack teacher in those days—fire in
the belly. Couldn't get him to stop talking about biology, even over
a beer. Things change though. Eventually, if, like Joe, you teach long
enough, most people don't even remember your name or what you
teach. So you tire."

He paused and then went on, "In Joe's early years he had a dream.
He wanted to go to Alaska and take pictures and then produce slides
of the flora and fauna for his classes. Well, several of Joe's close
friends are going to Alaska on a hunting trip this coming September,
and they have asked Joe to come along with his cameras. But Joe's
personal leave-time is all used up. He used those days when his wife
was hospitalized. Ray, would you meet with Joe and several of us from
the association to see if we can help him?" I agreed.

Later, the association leadership, Joe, and I met after school in my
office. Joe explained his situation. We deliberated. Our deliberation
was resolving nothing. The peaceful meeting was becoming tense.
Joe politely got up and headed for the door. He turned and said, "I'm
sorry, I didn't mean to cause such a problem." I then said something I
had not planned. I can only assume that I was guided in my statement
by a power greater than me. "Joe, wait. I have four unused personal

business days. Take mine." We were all stunned, including me. I turned to Bill. "Will the contract let me do this, Bill?" Bill slowly replied. "I'm not sure. Let us look into it."

They left shortly thereafter. Several days later Bill called. "Ray, we won't need your days, but we do need your assistance. The association leadership has decided to add a new provision to our contract permitting teachers to exchange unused personal leave days. Will you take this to the school board so that they can sign off on it?" "Be happy to, Bill."

Joe went to Alaska with his friends. He did so with five personal leave days given to him by his fellow teachers. He took his pictures of the flora and fauna and created his set of slides. After his return, our school board president asked him to present a portion of his slides at a school board meeting. His presentation was fascinating. He ended with these words. "It's been very long since my work has been so honored. Thank you."

Some say that Joe's last two years of teaching were his best. He taught with a "fire in the belly" that captivated his students and brought rookie teachers to him for guidance. His career ended not with a whimper but with an explosion of excitement. His career ended with honor—as all careers should.

*I was serving as the school superintendent. A group of teachers approached me and requested that they, along with parents, be permitted to create the first public charter school in Indiana.*

# Can You Help Us Create?

~

T HEIR ENTHUSIASM HAD NOTHING TO do with challenging the effectiveness of the current system. Rather, they believed that an alternative school might enhance what we could offer to a community with differing needs and interests. I, along with a visionary school board, agreed to support their effort. We then backed away and let them design their school, allowing and encouraging their artistic design to unfold. Three years later, Discovery School opened with an enrollment of 160 and a waiting list of nearly 90.

This school was established without incurring any financial burden to the district. It was enthusiastically supported by the union and teachers throughout the district, and it remained under the umbrella of the existing district. Parents and community members had been involved in its design and mission.

Most importantly, this school was not viewed as a competitor for students. Nor was it viewed as being better than the existing schools. It was viewed simply as a different way to respond to the unique needs and interests of a significant number of community parents and their children.

Some years later, a coalition of professional educators came to my home in Bloomington and met with me and teachers from that Discovery School. They asked how best to proceed with a state-wide charter school system. I offered the following advice: First, never create a state-wide system. Only local teachers and parents should initiate and develop such schools. The process should never be the result of a top-down plan designed by a school board, administration, or legislative body. Top-down ventures rarely have the ownership or creativity essential for success. Second, if this additional school results in an increasing cost to the district, then its existence will create anger and resentment within the broader community. Additional cost is, therefore, not an option. Third, the school must have extensive support from the broader community of teachers and parents.

These guidelines were virtually ignored. Instead, government officials and special interest groups such as The American Legislative Executive Council (ALEC) became deeply involved, distorted the charter concept, and created legislation with adversarial intent. The legislation had at its core the premise that American public education had failed. The charter school's evolving implementation predictably created deep divisions within the American community.

As I had warned, we now see and hear at the local level everywhere, angry and hateful discourse among well-intentioned, good people on both sides as they argue over the legality, character, and value of charter schools vs. the local public schools. Sadly, children and teachers in these environments are caught up in this cross-fire and have become collateral damage as they are often confused and worried about the educational choices that have been made for them.

There is only one way to resolve this destructive environment. This can only happen with the removal of the legislators responsible for enacting the laws and procedures which establish and protect charter schools in this deliberately distorted form.

Once this is accomplished, newly elected legislators must reverse the actions that have turned our communities into battlegrounds. We can then once again support our public schools and the teachers who have the willingness to find ways to enhance learning for all of our children. Our salvation so far is that our teachers, our classroom artists, have not left us. Despite the wars being waged, they wait patiently for the time when they can again walk into a superintendent's office and ask, "Can you help us create?"

*He was a coal miner from southern Indiana and he played a mean bass. He worked in the mines, studied nights, and played in a jazz band. Eventually he went to college and secured a doctorate at Ball State University. His name was Gary Phillips.*

# PROFOUND COMPLEXITY

~

I MET GARY WHILE HE WAS consulting for the Kettering/Lilly Foundations. This was during the time that Dean Evans served as the Indiana State Superintendent. In addition to Gary's many accomplishments, he was a gifted keynote speaker. Years ago, he gave a keynote address to the school administrators and many teachers of the Chicago Public Schools. From my notes and from my memory of that event, I describe his address below.

First, he started talking about a high school he knew well, telling about an early morning incident that had taken place in the school parking lot. The principal had turned away a carload of armed white adults intent on entering the school to harm several black students. Gary told about a second incident where immediately after school two girls who were in a bathroom were forced to give all of their cash to several older, stronger girls. One girl resisted. Then she was struck in the face and forced to take off all of her clothing. When found, she was hysterical.

He finally told about a junior boy who, on the same day, threatened to kill a teacher. The following morning the police searched him as he attempted to enter the building and removed a loaded revolver from his jacket pocket. Gary completed his description of the school with additional stories in the same vein. When he finished, the audience of some 1500 conference participants was quiet and sober.

He then told his audience about a second high school. He described the school salutatorian, a young woman, captain of her soccer team, who had recently accepted a full academic scholarship to Columbia University. He added that an additional four top scholars of the senior class had also accepted full academic scholarships to other Ivy League schools. He continued to note outstanding student achievements: the chess club taking third place in a national tournament, the band finishing second in a state competition, the girls basketball team winning first place in their division for the third consecutive year. For the next ten minutes, he continued to share stories regarding the accomplishments of many other talented and committed students. When he finished he asked, "Which school would you want your son or daughter to attend?" The answer was so obvious most in the audience, perplexed, sat quietly.

Then Gary continued, "The answer is not so simple or apparent, for what I did not tell you was that the first school and the second school are actually the same school, and all of the incidents that I have described took place in that same school.

It is a school of academic excellence, a school of profoundly difficult problems, a school of winning moments, and of moments that occasionally border on disaster. It is a school that can become better, and a school that must become better. It is, in many respects, the school in your own community. It is, as are all schools, a school that defies a simple grade of A, B, C, D, or F. It is too complex to be judged so simplistically. Like all schools, it is a changing, living, breathing entity that good teachers, committed students, parents, and dedicated principals everywhere try to make better every day.

Don't devalue it by trying to assign some simple label or grade to it. Rather, recognize it as the profound complexity that it is. Then cherish and support it."

*Carnivals at one time had a magician who was a master of sleight of hand. He would have three shells on a small table and under one of the shells would be an object, often a bean or coin. He would show you under which shell he put the object. Then he would move the shells around and around and ask you to select the shell under which the object rested. Of course he had removed the bean or coin before moving the shells. Thus he always got you to choose inappropriately. The following suggests a fairly sophisticated shell game that all of us have been asked to buy into.*

# THE SHELL GAME

⁓

E VERY YEAR PRESEASON COLLEGE FOOTBALL magazines are
published. Contained within them is a list of teams expected to
rank in the top 25 in the nation. In the current *Athlon Football Preview*
this list includes the perennially highly successful teams: Alabama,
Ohio State, Florida State, Georgia, USC, Penn State, Clemson,
Oklahoma, Auburn, Michigan, Notre Dame, and LSU. A second list
ranks the top recruiting classes including, not surprisingly, Alabama,
Ohio State, Georgia, USC, Penn State, Clemson, Oklahoma, Auburn,
Michigan, Norte Dame, and LSU.

It appears obvious that those teams who are most successful at
recruiting are also the most successful at winning. Some might say,
"Wait, isn't the quality of coaching the major factor in winning?" Not
really. While good coaching is extremely important, it is a fact that the
men who coach the 130 Division I teams are all very competent, very
hard working, and tend to excel at what they do. But it is recruiting
that is the most reliable variable. Interesting shell game? How about
the following.

Annually, K-12 standardized test scores are published in
communities across the country. No matter where you live, certain
schools every year score at the top and others each year score at the
bottom. Does this happen because some schools have only good
teachers, some only bad teachers? Not really. With few exceptions
the teachers in most schools are, like those coaches, very competent,
very hard working, and tend to excel at what they do. So, do certain

schools recruit better? No, no. That's football. For these schools, the variable that makes the difference is the wealth of the community. Invariably, greater wealth results in significantly higher test scores. Were we again talked into selecting the wrong shell?

So why do the print media devote columns and columns to reporting these results which only result in perpetuating the myth? Why do they not more forcefully examine what would be truly informative? Conservatively, including the loss of teacher instruction time, our nation is spending well over five billion dollars a year on this shell game. What if we used that money to finally adequately fund special education, or to focus on the real issues teachers face, or to simply pay teachers a better salary?

Some might ask if we abandon standardized testing, how will we know the things we need to know about children? How will we know how well they are achieving? How will we know their deficiencies? How will universities and the communities at large know that they are prepared to join adult society or go on to higher education?

The answer is simple. We should do as we had done for so long— we should ask their teachers. The knowledge that teachers have regarding their students goes far, far beyond what standardized tests report or are capable of reporting.

There was a time when we accepted this. We asked teachers for their guidance and wisdom. If you have forgotten or were never aware of this, pull from your saved family treasures the graduation diploma of your parents, grandparents, or great grandparents. Read the ancient text on those diplomas which declared this professional judgment: "At the recommendation of the Faculty." Notice that no standardized score is cited. It was a time when we trusted and honored teacher judgment.

*His name was Tom. He was a student in my government class. He possessed a provocative depth of inquiry not found in most his age.*

# A Christmas Card

~

ON A COLD, FRIDAY AFTERNOON in February, we were studying the disparity of wealth existing among nations. I could see that Tom was thinking intensely about the topic, yet he did not participate. He said nothing. Finally, I said to him, "Tom, what are you thinking?" He looked up and somewhat apologetically said, "I'd rather not say." I gently persisted. Tom answered. His response was neither adversarial nor challenging.

He simply said, "Mr. Golarz, there's no morality in the world." His response was clearly not cognitive, but rather a response that seemed to come from someplace deep inside of his soul. Had it been cognitive, I would have debated. But his response was clearly more in the manner of a core value. So I simply said, "Tom, I disagree." Soon class was over. I sat in the faculty lounge lamenting that I did not have the skill to dissuade him of his position. I felt, as teachers often do, that I had failed him. Where was the magic of wisdom?

Several weeks later there was a scheduled exam. Three students, including Tom, missed the exam. Tom's absence was for a reason that did not require my permitting a makeup exam. Several days later, as students were leaving class, I asked Tom to wait. When we were alone, I said, "Tom, I'll be in the building late tomorrow if you would like to come by and make up the exam, I'll be here." He looked surprised and said, "That's awfully nice of you, Mr. Golarz."

The next thing I said I hadn't planned. I said, "Tom, it's simply the moral thing to do." He looked stunned. I continued, "Will you be there?" After a long moment, he said quietly and slowly, "Yes, Sir. I'll be there."

Tom took his exam. We never discussed my comment. Several months later he graduated. Six months after graduation, I received a phone call near midnight, "Mr. Golarz, this is Tom. Do you think we could have coffee and talk?" A half hour later we met at George's Diner in East Chicago. We drank coffee and talked all night. At 7 a.m., I shaved in the faculty lounge and went to teach. Later, we met again, and again we talked most of the night. Soon thereafter we lost contact. I learned years later that he had been severely wounded in military action and decorated for valor.

I heard no more of Tom until recently. My wife Marion usually opens our Christmas cards. One evening while reading the cards she asked, "Who's Tom?" At first I didn't remember, but then I realized that "Tom" was the former student I had shared those long conversations with so many years ago.

He wrote, "This Christmas thank-you note is long overdue. I'm an engineer in California now and many evenings I coach basketball for wheelchair-handicapped kids. One of my kids who also struggles emotionally and wanted to give up recently asked me, "Coach, why do you give me so many chances?" I wanted to tell him that it was "simply the moral thing to do," but I'm not sure he would have understood. I know, however, that you will understand. So thanks, Mr. Golarz."

I treasure that card as only teachers do. We hear too infrequently that we made a difference, but differences are made by teachers every day. No teacher should ever forget that.

*For many years, I worked daily in the impoverished communities of Northwest Indiana and South Chicago. I got to know the culture and the community idiosyncrasies house- by-house, alleyway-by-alleyway, and neighborhood-by-neighborhood. I became familiar with the odors, the loss of hope, the depression, the tears, and the brutality that overshadowed the occasional joys.*

# CYNTHIA

~

PRIOR TO MY LONG WORK with these communities, I thought naively that some people were simply poor. The longer I worked, the more I came to understand that there were no less than two kinds of poor—the poor and the very poor. My daily immersion in their lives gave me a deeper understanding of the endless burdens of those who made up the very poor.

I found as I worked that their lives were desperate not simply because they had no money and few resources, but because they were trapped. Life without viable supports or options had crushed and permanently changed them.

Cynthia was one of the many people I got to know who were among the desperately poor. I first met her when I responded to a neighborhood alert advising that someone might be living in an old, abandoned clapboard garage.

It was mid-January when I cautiously worked my way over ice and snow covered walkways to the backyard structure. The garage door was slightly ajar. I knocked. I knocked again. The door opened slightly. Through this slightly opened doorway I could see a frail and small woman wrapped in a torn blanket. Only her lower legs were exposed and there appeared to be snakes wrapped around and moving on those exposed lower legs. She looked so very sad, cold, and pathetic.

Behind her in the back corner of the garage I could see a cot covered with old rags. There was movement under the rags. As my eyes became more accustomed to the darkness, I could see that the movement was being caused by small children. They were making no noise, simply huddling together attempting to stay warm. Within the garage there were only two sources of light. A single light hanging down from an electrical cord and an opening at the bottom of the back wall where insufficient rags were allowing daylight along with snow to enter the room. I saw then that the snakes on her legs were actually large varicose veins. It is strange how such sights never leave you. Though this occurred many years ago, these images remain burned in my psyche. I later came to know that she had seven children. She was but 23 that cold January day.

As I began to work with Cynthia and her children, I came to know them. One of the first things Cynthia confided to me was that one of her earliest, most terrifying memories was of being repeatedly raped at the age of seven. She thought that these assaults had actually occurred much earlier, but she wasn't sure. She told me that she learned through those experiences never to fight back or resist, for to do so would only result in more beatings. Vulnerable and helpless, she had learned to become quiet.

The eldest of five siblings herself, it was Cynthia's job to tend to the younger ones when her mother was gone. Her schooling didn't even begin until about the fifth grade when a case worker for the Department of Public Welfare found her foraging for food in the neighborhood alleyways, thus revealing her pathetic existence. At age 13 she had her first child, never sure of who the father was. As she spoke, she tried not to smile for her teeth were rotting very badly and some had fallen out.

Cynthia was one of the most timid persons I have ever known. Seldom did she raise her eyes when talking to you. She knew virtually nothing beyond the four-square-block area where she had been born and lived her life. She was illiterate and ignorant about so many things. She knew nothing of her entitlements as a person, much less as an American.

She did not know where welfare or food stamps came from. She was often filled with fear, so when she encountered anyone in authority, she was always afraid that she might say something that would cause her meager benefits to be terminated.

Cynthia and so many like her—the extremely poor—would never have the personal confidence or knowledge to understand and pursue social benefits for herself or her children. She did not know of networks that might help.

Only strong local, state, and federal support systems might, with immense and consistent hard work, pull people like Cynthia's out of this disempowering poverty and restore them to sufficient strength and will to get appropriate help. But such systems, as we all know, do not exist. What does exist is a system of overworked, understaffed, and underpaid welfare workers.

This inadequate social welfare system, coupled with the permanently debilitating nature of this kind of poverty, makes fools of those wealthier citizens who assume that all poor people are equally capable of participation in programs meant to change their lives. Tragically, there is little understanding that there exists an American caste system with the very, very poor clinging to the bottom rung of that system's ladder with no viable way out.

Cynthia died of Pneumonia and deprivation at age 25.

*During the 60s and 70s, many of us were engaged, we thought, in crushing forever racial prejudice and injustice. Our marches, protests, legislation, and writings were all so aimed. We were convinced in the end that we had made substantial progress and so we rested. We neglected to understand that there were others exhaling their breath of hate on a new generation that was breathing it in. Thus, we learned that if the war were to be won, we could never leave the battlefield. The racial war and its direct and collateral damage continue to rage. Following is a selection of short stories describing such damage.*

# THE ENDLESS WAR

~

**A** COLLEAGUE HAD JUST BECOME A **superintendent in the Deep South**. He asked me to come and speak to the teachers in his district. I agreed. Several weeks later as I was disembarking the plane, I was met by my friend. As we walked to his car he asked if I wouldn't mind allowing him to show me his bus garage. I was tired and it seemed an unusual request, but I assumed he must have a good reason for making such a request.

We got to the bus garage area and then we drove back and forth row, after row, after row. I finally said, "Ray, I didn't think your school district was this big." He replied, "It isn't. We don't bus the whites with the blacks."

**I was working in the inner-city schools of Chicago.** One afternoon I was in the library talking with a group of middle school children. We talked for over an hour. One of the girls seemed intensely focused upon me. When we finished I said to her, "You seemed to be watching me very closely." She smiled and said, "I was." She then added, "I've never seen a white man in the real, just on television. I'm so glad you're nice."

**I invited Dr. Oliver to lunch.** He had been my favorite college professor. He graciously accepted. We went to the Riviera Lounge. It was close to the college. We sat in a booth in the bar area. The conversation was easy. What he didn't know about biology wasn't worth knowing. We were waiting a very long time.

I excused myself and went to the bartender/owner. I said, "Excuse me, Mickey. We seem to be waiting a very long time." He looked straight into my eyes and responded, "Get the N***** out of here." Rage engulfed me. I started to reach for him when from behind me an arm grabbed mine. I turned back and looked into the eyes of Dr. Oliver who said to me. "Ray, please, no. Please."

**The first graders from three inner city schools screamed with delight as their field trip busses were approaching downtown Chicago.** I asked, "Is downtown that exciting?" Dr. Phedonia Johnson, Director of CANAL, the Chicago desegregation project replied, "No, it's not downtown Chicago that has them so excited. You see, Ray, the neighborhoods that they live in are dominated by rival gangs, so if these young children leave their neighborhoods, they are not safe. They are that excited because they are looking at the trees lining these downtown Chicago streets. Many of them have never seen living trees before."

**My wife and I had been at a party for teachers.** When we left, rather than going home we went to a restaurant /bar near Chicago that we understood was often frequented by teachers. We went with a teacher friend named Otto who taught English literature. We were sitting and enjoying one another's company when a stranger came up behind Otto and whispered something we couldn't hear. Otto excused himself and left with the stranger. I became uneasy. I asked myself, "Who would Otto know in this area of Chicago?"

I told Marion that I was going to look for him and asked her to wait. At the back of the restaurant area near a dance floor not then in use, I saw Otto surrounded by seven or eight white men. I approached and asked, "Everything all right?" One of the larger men turned to me and asked, "You the one who brought this N***** in here?" I glanced at Otto who appeared terrified. I responded, "Yes, we are teachers." He replied, "Not very bright teachers, are ya?" As he spoke, he began punching me in the chest with his right closed fist—hard enough to cause me to continue to fall back.

He said, "you're a N***** lover, aren't ya?'" I did not raise my fists or act in any aggressive manner. I could see in Otto's eyes a plea for my restraint. The other men slowly followed, laughing and jeering as they did. Eventually, they pushed both Otto and me out into the street with a warning. I got Marion and we all left.

Marion and I thought about that incident for a long time. We reflected on the humiliation of our friend Otto, the fear we felt, the unfairness of it all. We knew that while we had escaped physical brutality that night, we had not escaped the ugliness borne out of ignorance and hate.

*Don Sims, a Native American Chief, was the administrative head of Riverside Indian School in Oklahoma. Over the years we had become close friends. Don's never ending commitment was to find ways to instill pride in Native American children.*

# GAAGII

~

As chief administrator he oversaw the building of a basketball gym. Donning his coaching cap, he took his Riverside kids to third place in the state tournament. In his third year he changed the academic report card. The grade of F was eliminated and replaced with the grade NY (not yet). Don told everyone, "No child fails here. We simply give them more time." His returning dropout center was a work of art. It was personally built by Don, his teachers and returning dropouts. They called it "New Home." Few dropped out again.

One of Don's most prized projects, designed to instill pride in his students, was the one he worked out with *USA Today*. He arranged for each pupil—400 plus—to receive that paper every day. These students would find on the address bar their name, identifying them as the paper's intended recipient. Afterwards, walking through Don's campus was a real treasure as one could observe young men and women sitting in a favorite corner quietly reading. It is for me a very special memory.

Sadly, this uniquely empowering experience which had brought such pleasure would eventually result in profound shame to one of these proud students. It was mid-January when Don asked me to come to Riverside. I got there and went immediately to his office. His normal demeanor of strength and optimism had faded. He asked me to sit and then slowly told me a story that one of his 14-year-old Navajo students, Gaagii Nez, had shared with him.

Gaagii related to Don that he had never been as proud as when he received his *USA Today* newspaper. His name was on the paper—not handwritten but actually printed in the address bar. He had never before seen his name in print. He saved the paper to take to his grandfather Niyoi, Chief of his tribe in Arizona. They would look at it together, this first of his newspapers, and both would be proud.

It would not be until December that he would take the bus ride from Oklahoma to Arizona and his home. There was a stop in Flagstaff and he got off. He needed to use the bathroom. As he left the bus, he carried only his treasured newspaper.

No sooner had he finished going to the bathroom and washing his hands when two big white men came in. The bigger of the two looked down at Gaagii and said, "Hey, Indian, gimme that G**damn newspaper." Gaagii told Don that he grasped his paper tight, looked up nervously and replied, "It is mine." "Give it here, Indian. Probably can't read anyway." Then both men laughed. Gaagii told Don that he sensed danger and tried to run and escape, but they were too big and blocked his way. In the brief fight that ensued, his newspaper was shredded. As he lay on the bathroom floor, he could hear the men as they left, "Damn paper isn't even today's."

He then crawled to the urinal where parts of his newspaper lay. He found the label with his name and picked it up. It was stained with urine and getting wet now from his own tears falling quietly from his face. He felt such shame. How would he tell Niyoi?

Don looked up, tears now streaming slowly down his face. "Why, Ray, why?"

I could think of nothing that would provide comfort, so we just sat there together in the silence of his office.

*When I was a child in school, every six weeks I got a report card that I had to take home and have signed by my parents. I was given three grades in each subject. One grade for academic progress, one grade for my effort, and the final and most important grade was for conduct. The conduct grades were the first grades that my parents looked at, for these conduct grades advised them as to my behavior, my civility, and my ability to get along with and see the unique needs of my fellow man. If the conduct grades were low, there was usually a short note written by the teacher in an appropriate place on the report card.*

*In the days of my growing-up, both parents and teachers saw these virtues as essential and primary. Their hope was that their teaching and guidance would result in the acquisition of such virtues. The following story is intended to illustrate what happens when parents and teachers are successful. When teachers and parents get it right, what does success look like? This true story comes from the great depression only days before Christmas of 1933.*

# THE CHRISTMAS PURSE

~

MARY WAS THE ONLY ONE of her family employed. She did housework. It was Friday near 7 p.m. Outside a winter blizzard was raging. Two of her sons were preparing to go out and look for her. She was never this late. At that moment heavy pounding resounded at the back kitchen door. Lefty, the eldest son, rushed to the door, opened it and Mary, his mother, covered with snow and ice, fell onto the kitchen floor. She was bleeding from her hands, knees and forehead. Her hands and scarfless head felt frozen. Her family tended to her as she tearfully shared her story.

She had left work clutching her change purse containing her week's wages of $3.70, money essential for her family's Christmas dinner. Somewhere along the railroad tracks that she walked to get back to her neighborhood, she lost her purse. For two hours, often on her hands and knees, she searched in vain along those tracks. Donning heavy clothing, Lefty and Mickey assured her they would find her purse. They departed, heading for the tracks. On their way, they encountered several of their football teammates and told them what was going on.

The blizzard was intensifying. Despite their flashlights, the half-mile stretch of track they searched appeared black because of the heavy, wind-driven snow. The flashlights were virtually useless. Back and forth along the entire stretch of track they walked slowly while continually squinting and wiping their freezing eyes. An hour passed. Hands freezing, they again reversed course.

Now in the distance they saw several lights. A train? No, not bright enough. The approaching lights got brighter. Through the storm from the distant lights someone yelled out, "Lefty. Lefty, that you and Mickey?" "That you, Cal?" "Yeah, me and most of the team. The two of you didn't think we were gonna let you stroll in this evening delight without us, did ya?" "You guys didn't have to...." "Shut up, Lefty, just lead and we will follow with our lights." For the next three hours they searched—back and forth along the tracks. It was nearing midnight and the storm had continued to intensify.

Then Cal screamed, "We found it." Lefty and Mickey turned and rushed back. When they reached Cal and the team, they could see through the snow in Cal's cupped hands, a mix of coins—mostly pennies, nickels, and other small change. "It's only three dollars and sixty one cents. Somewhere your ma lost nine cents. "Cal, we can't take your money." Cal replied, "Isn't for you, Lefty. It's for a mother sitting in her living room and praying that her sons will find her Christmas purse."

At one o'clock that morning, Mary was given the money. She knew it wasn't hers. Her purse had three dollar bills, two quarters and two dimes. She resisted, but it was useless for they would not relent.

The different backgrounds of this beloved team of gift-givers were many. Some had attended public schools—others parochial. Some were of immigrant families and some were of families of longer American duration. Their ethnic and racial origins were varied.

Their commonalities were compassion, civility and poverty. The poverty, however, was empty pockets only—never empty hearts. They had been taught in their homes and schools to open their hearts to those in need. You see, when teachers and parents get it right, this is what success can look like.

The little change purse was never found.

*Evenings, in homes across this great land, children sit at kitchen tables struggling with academic content that their parents and they have been told is essential to know if they are going to score high on standardized tests. The atmosphere in the house is again tense and the momentary respite at day's end, essential to good mental health is gone—preempted by this insanity.*

*On those same tense evenings, a tired teacher reworks the lesson for tomorrow. Her constant question is, "Will this help with the upcoming standardized test?" Invariably this question is followed by another question, "How long can I continue this?"*

# Madness

~

U SING STANDARDIZED TESTS TO ASSESS a student's level of achievement is the game of politicians, not of local school boards, teachers, or parents. The lives that American parents and teachers want for children are filled rather with an array of richness and growth in a multitude of areas. Doing well in school is important. But they also want their children to taste, enjoy, and grow from so much more.

They want them to lie in a grassy field on a summer day and read a novel for pleasure, know the sound of Bach, enjoy rap, and share in the caring of an elderly grandparent. They want them to enjoy and be proud of their capacity to manipulate new technologies, play in a football game, run a race, attend a prom, and gain skills with the many tools that they find in their family garage and kitchen.

They want them to take pride in and understand the history of their own race and ethnicity, sense and then respond to the needs of their fellow man, know the thrill of hitting a home run and glory in the skill of controlling a soccer ball, knee-to-knee-to-toe-to-knee. They want them to babysit a neighbor's child and earn their own dollar, have time to reflect on the world's new discoveries, get a little choked up at the playing of their own national anthem, and waste away an afternoon playing basketball with friends in a park.

If this means that some nation with less freedom and less true breadth and depth of knowing outscores them on some artificial measure of greatness, then so be it. These tests measure such a very narrow band of knowing and being. They really measure nothing of the greatness of a people, nor of their potential for greatness.

And if our children find that they need to compete at the highest levels for something that they really want, they will. They always have. Just give them a fair and level competitive field. Then when they come to you, interview them, face-to-face. Never substitute knowing them with a test score. Give them half a fighting chance and they will come the rest of the way.

Throw away your state and national standardized tests. Get back to knowing who these children really are. All these tests do is obscure their unique value and potential greatness.

*I did my student teaching at Hammond Technical Vocational High School. One day the principal, Mr. Wilson, invited me to lunch in his office.*

# ARTISTRY

~

I N HIS OFFICE WAS A large book case filled with black bound volumes. Each volume identified a subject matter course offered during the Great Depression. He explained, "During those times students would often need to drop out and go to work. Upon returning, they came back to a set of F's for courses never completed. Discouraged, they left. In order to remedy this condition, we teachers structured all of our courses with content sections.

Thus, if students had to drop out, they were given a report card showing the number of sections completed and the number remaining. Upon returning to school, they would simply finish the remaining sections. Failure would not occur again for the children of depression-era poverty." I asked, "Why did you stop?" He replied, "The state declared that our strategy was somehow violating their standards. I keep these volumes to remind myself of an earlier, more flexible and empathetic time."

I received a phone call from a superintendent in Illinois. He called to inquire about our school district's very successful kindergarten intervention program. He suggested that he wanted to send a team of administrators to study our effort, and if the team found it to be a "best practice," they would implement it.

I responded, "Sir, a specific or predesigned model has little to do with the program's success. The creative implementation and on-going modifications are all in the hands of the teachers. The extraordinary success is due to the continuous hard work and creativity of that staff. I hate to see you waste a trip." He responded, "Well then, how do you administratively maintain control?" I said, "You don't." We ended our conversation. He never called back.

Artists must control the art. I taught seventh grade history as I was taught: first student, stand and read; second student, stand and read; third student, and so on. My students were not really learning or understanding much history.

One day I said to a student, "Come up to the chalkboard and make a mark at the far left end indicating the arrival of Columbus in 1492. Then, assuming the entire front chalkboard is all of American history, make a mark for the signing of the Constitution." About three feet from her first mark, she made the second mark. Then I asked her to mark where we are now. She placed this mark at the end of the chalkboard some twenty feet away. Students became curious and engaged. One student suggested that we allow one inch for each year. When we did, we were all stunned. The period from 1492 to the Constitution filled the entire chalkboard.

The adjoining chalkboard was needed to represent history to the present time. In the following weeks, suggestions for added information came quickly—a line for famous persons, another line for inventions, and a line representing population growth. History, in their hands, was becoming alive.

Some years ago, Marion and I were watching *Back stage at Lincoln Center* on PBS. Zubin Mehta was being interviewed with respect to the qualities essential for conducting. He spoke of how he watched the artists as they watched him until at some point in the performance they tell him with a knowing look to let go. He does so, and at that point the music becomes their own. He, the conductor, simply holds them together.

Great teaching is a daily creative art. It occurs in environments where the artist feels free and trusted to create. Why would we want it any other way?

*Stephen Gould's The Mismeasure of Man opens by presenting a dialogue between Socrates and Glaucon wherein they fabricate a myth. The myth suggests that God had framed people differently—bright people (commanders), average people (auxiliaries), and dull people (husbandmen and craftsmen). Socrates and Glaucon then agree that the Greek citizenry would never believe such an absurd myth. However they speculate, "But their sons may be made to believe, and their son's sons and posterity after them."*

# MYTHOLOGY

~

A RE WE THAT POSTERITY? HAVE we structured our institutions including education to mirror and support the myth?

Early in the twentieth century, a test was created called the Stanford-Binet. Over time it became viewed as the definitive measure of human intelligence even though this was not the designer's original intent. The test, administered individually, became the standard by which other intelligence tests were judged. But does the Binet or any of the other "intelligence" tests really measure intelligence?

Although test results highly correlate with proficiencies in math and language arts, the results do not also correlate highly with empathy, civility, musical skills, and artistic capacities—capacities which also reflect intelligence. Might all of these tests simply be measuring academic achievement—academic achievement that we all know is tied to wealth and opportunity?

Beginning in the 1980s, researchers like Howard Gartner in his *Frames of Mind*, and Daniel Goleman in his *Emotional Intelligence*, began to seriously challenge the very narrow kind of intelligence definition being promoted. For a time these researchers had a profound impact on the way intelligence was defined and assessed.

Their work had a significant effect, especially on the way teaching methods were modified to broaden instructional strategies, notably at the primary and secondary levels. Their work also prompted many in the business community to look beyond academic grades in a resume.

Tragically, beginning with the unprecedented move to make our students "more competitive" with students in other countries, we have reverted to the use of very narrow standardized testing to define what we will accept as evidence of gradations of intelligence. We have come seriously close to accepting the myth that Socrates and Glaucon had proposed and feared would come to be. (1)

As a young teacher, I once taught all seniors whose total class was divided into seven academic levels. The entire senior class had been tested using a group intelligence test that highly correlated with math and language art skills. Throughout the day I taught different levels. For example, the first period might consist of a group of level four students and second period might consist of a group of level six students.

My daily teaching experiences clearly were a contradiction to this supposition of gradation. For example, I recall a distraught senior girl who was placed in the level one group, supposedly the smartest group. One day, this senior girl came to me in tears, having failed miserably an essay type exam. The exam had required that she be able to think critically and respond logically to questions over material we had been studying.

"Please, Mr. Golarz, just give me a multiple choice exam. I have everything memorized." In other observations I found many students who possessed proficiencies that contradicted their assigned level. My finest art student, for example, was a level six despite the fact that artistic achievement requires considerable intellectual abilities.

In later years as an administrator, I directed gifted education as well as special education. The one constant observation I made in those years was that many young people had been misplaced and mislabeled. Often children who had been labeled as gifted were simply lost when asked to engage in complex projects. The greatest tragedy, however, was to find children who had lost their capacity to believe in themselves because they had come to believe in the demeaning label placed on them by some paper and pencil test.

Intelligence is never a narrow cognitive thing. Only when we understand and enhance both the discrete skills and the full range of everyone's intellectual potential will we discover and reap the benefits of the gifts that allow us all to attain greatness. There are not preordained commanders, auxiliaries, and craftsmen—there is simply a world filled with a wide diversity of people God has created who possess an array of incredible gifts of differing types and sizes.

Is it not time for us to set the myth aside, for it continues to obstruct our seeing one another properly—of seeing the potential sensitivity, deep understanding, and intuitive thought that exists in us all.

1 Golarz and Golarz, *The Problem Isn't Teachers*, Section Five: The War Over Purpose, pp 138-152.

*One of my administrative assignments was to oversee the dropout problem. The school district had nearly 23,000 students. Annually we lost nearly 500. Despite our efforts only about 200 returned. We would then rent an old, vacant, downtown storefront facility and employ specialized staff. Within a month a full 70% of those returning would again drop out. Large school districts throughout our country were experiencing the same thing. Our lack of success was frustrating.*

# BELIEVE IN ME

~

A T A CONFERENCE IN PHOENIX, Dr. Gary Phillips explained that some years earlier this national problem of reoccurring dropouts did not occur in Seattle for a span of several years. Returning dropouts were staying at an 80% level. He explained further. The Seattle public schools had not been able to find a suitable downtown facility, so contractual arrangements were made with the University of Washington to rent several of their classrooms.

Soon neighbors of these dropouts throughout the city were asking, "Where are you going with those books? Thought you had dropped out of school." The returning students proudly replied, "My classes are at the University of Washington now." What had Seattle inadvertently tied into? What serendipity?

Sometime later I was presenting at a conference in Tulsa regarding the power of belief systems. At the break, one of Tulsa's assistant superintendents asked to share a story. When we resumed she began. As a young teacher of special education at the elementary school level, she challenged her students to believe in themselves. She told them to dream, for only through challenging dreams could they succeed.

After school one of her students, a little girl, timidly came to her. "Teacher, I have a dream, but I'm afraid." "Why, child, are you afraid?" "I'm not smart like other children, so my dream is foolish." "Never say that. Tell me about your dream, and I will help you." The young child then said, "I want to win the school spelling bee." The assistant superintendent shared with us the terror she felt. Had she set this beautiful child up for failure—this child whose eyes and heart were now filled with hope? How could she tell this child that her dream was not attainable? She couldn't.

For the next nine weeks every day after school and on weekends, she dedicated herself to assisting this child and her mother in preparing for the contest all the while convinced that failure and tragedy were looming. The night before the competition, she confessed to us that she did not sleep.

Then came the competition. The final round of the competition was the most difficult for her to watch. Would it—could it really happen? Then the miracle occurred. The child with an impossible dream won, and from this little girl she heard, "I won because I knew that you knew that I could. I knew it in my heart." Weeks later at the city competition, she didn't get eliminated until the fifth round.

Years ago, Charles Horton Cooley created a concept titled "The Looking Glass Self." Fundamentally, the concept suggests that *who I am* is a combination of *who I think I am*, *who you think I am*, and *who I think you think I am*. Much of the essence of a child's identity rests with us. Do they believe that we believe in them? How do they know? Do we house them in an old, vacant, downtown storefront, or in an edifice that is elegant and gives them a feeling of dignity?

Do we fail to inspire them, or do we empower them by showing them how to chase after their dreams?

Children become the manifestation of the dreams that they believe we dream with them before they dream of succeeding in the dreams of their own.

*Not long ago Marion and I co-authored a book titled The Problem Isn't Teachers. Throughout the text we emphasized that the conditions of poverty and the demise of the American middle class have been the principal underlying causes for the declining effectiveness of America's public schools.*

# JUSTICE

~

Although we discussed in detail additional contributing factors such as inadequate special education funding and erroneous Supreme Court decisions, poverty and wage inequality were the principle causes of declining effectiveness. Proof of our position is easily secured by simply observing the strong correlation that exists in all parts of our country between neighborhood poverty and the lack of student academic success in such neighborhoods.

An understanding of this reality makes legislative actions such as tying teacher performance and pay to student achievement or the practice of the grading of schools absurd and tragic. Even more disastrous is our unwillingness to accept what needs to be done. Poverty and inequality are the issues. Do we have the national will to address these?

There is a myth that the poor are content to be poor. But, in fact, the poor abhor poverty. They also resent charity because such efforts provoke shame and feelings of inferiority and inequality. The poor, like the rest of mankind, need honor and justice. They need to feel proud and valued. Most importantly, they need to be recognized for their true worth.

Some time ago, President Obama changed the Department of Labor rule regarding overtime pay. The rule change, long overdue, made employees earning less than $47,500.00 eligible for overtime pay. This action changed the older standard of providing such earned overtime only to those earning no more than $23,660.00.

With this action over 4,000,000 working Americans would have been able to take a big step toward fairness, dignity, and the middle class, a step which has been denied to them for the past 40 years. Five to seven hundred dollars per month after taxes would have become available to each home. Thus, there would have been money from overtime pay to purchase a book for a child, or for a second pair of school shoes, or for a family meal at a restaurant other than McDonalds, or for a shopping trip with mom for a new spring coat at a store other than Goodwill.

But the new regulation was crushed. Quickly, businesses and even universities supported the demise of this effort and stripped justice from the hands of the American working-poor by abruptly halting these additional payments of fairly earned income.

All would soon return to the immoral normal, thus the prosperous citizens in our country could, once again, dutifully and comfortably support partially funded preschool programs, marginally funded food stamp programs, limited access to health care, food pantries, and clothing drives—all charitable things. They could return to feeling that they were doing enough.

As in the past, the wealthiest will be able to continue to support all of these things while they remain ignorant of the real needs of the poor. They will continue to fail to understand that the most important thing the poor long for and deserve is justice for their true worth.

The distance between charity and justice is infinite.

*Public schools in America, over their long history, have never been adequately funded. Consequently, when state-sponsored charter schools are approved, such approval spells a financial crisis for local school districts.*

# IMPOSSIBLE BURDEN

~

WHY AND HOW DOES THIS happen? Much of the financial support for charter schools comes from state funds earmarked for local districts. Money that would have been utilized for a public school child is taken away from the public school district.

Thus, if the local community schools have, for example, 480 individual classrooms and two children leave a third of these classrooms and enroll in the new charter, the loss to the community public schools would be approximately $5,500.00 dollars per pupil. If you multiply that dollar amount times the approximately 320 children who just left for the charter school, then the total loss to the district schools would be $1,760, 000.00 dollars.

Because a charter school typically does not receive entire classes of children from the sending schools, but rather only one or two or three per classroom, then the local school district has no way of responsibly reducing staff. How do you reduce staff when one class size changes from 28 to 26 and another change from 30 to28?

Further, because all school districts in the United States typically spend 85 to 90 percent of their total budget on staff costs, the loss to an already strapped and fiscally responsible school district as described above would be catastrophic.

"But wait," some say. "How about a referendum? If we were to vote to establish a referendum or to continue one, would that not fill this new financial deep hole?" Of course it would help, but think about what that means. Should we use newly secured referendum monies to fill an unanticipated new financial hole created, not by the community's established needs, but by a small number of community neighbors who believe that their new charter school is better than the schools established for and by the broader community?

Well, if we don't tap into referendum monies, then what? Do we reduce remedial reading support materials and teacher aides for some of our more needy children? Do we decrease staff medical benefits? Do we require all children engaged in extracurricular activities pay a participation fee? Do we reduce custodial and/or cafeteria staffs? How about counselors or social workers? How about the staffs that support our libraries? Where will we make the cuts?

America's public schools have never been adequately funded. To move the limited funds currently directed to public schools to charter schools is criminal and places an impossible burden on public schools.

*The tragedy of this story is that it is the story of thousands and thousands of hard working Americans.*

# STAN AND MARY

~

S TAN AND MARY WERE MARRIED in 1956. In 1953, Stan came home
from the Korean War and got a job working on the Lake Erie
docks in Cleveland. It was hard work, but he was delighted to have
the job. In 1957 Mary had their first child. Shortly thereafter, she was
pregnant with their second. A house become available in a modest
neighborhood they liked, and with the financial help of family, they
bought it.

The house had been constructed in 1938. It was well-built and
had a basement, kitchen, dining room, a small den, one bathroom,
and four bedrooms upstairs. It needed work, but it would be a home
where they could raise their family.

For the first five years after purchasing the house, they bought
only the essentials. With any money left over they paid back the
relatives who had assisted them with the purchase of the house
and also put aside money in the "strike fund." God forbid that the
dockworkers would go on strike, but if they did, they would need to
be ready.

Eventually, they had six children and they all attended the school
down the street, Roosevelt Elementary. It was a working-class school,
a school where parents and teachers worked together. Children
understood that violating standards would not be tolerated— not at
school or at home.

Over the years, Stan slowly improved their house. A second
bathroom was built in 1960 with the help of Mary's brother and

a friend who was a plumber. In 1963 Stan began remodeling the kitchen, giving Mary a double sink, a window that looked out over her back yard, cabinets, and a larger area for the kitchen table. He pretty much finished the kitchen in 1965. In addition, he rewired the basement, built bookshelves in the den, painted and replaced most of the front porch, and put in a two-car garage. With friends and relatives, he laid a concrete driveway on the side of the house which went all the way to the detached garage near the back of the lot. By the time Stan retired, there wasn't much that hadn't been rebuilt, repaired, or touched up.

After a long, good life together raising their family in that comfortable home, Mary passed away. Stan, shortly thereafter, kept getting confused, fell badly a couple of times, and then went several miles away to live with a daughter and her husband.

Stan and Mary hadn't saved a lot. They had spent their money frugally while raising a family. Stan had done most of the home improvements by himself or with family and friends. Mary had cooked, cleaned, and helped maintain the condition of their home while she tutored, nursed, and gave individualized attention to a growing and maturing family.

After Mary passed, Stan's only real asset was the house, and now the time had come to sell it. But he felt okay about that. He had kept it in good shape, and its reasonable sale would give to each of his six children a small inheritance while they raised their own children. So Stan and some of his children arranged a meeting at the house with a local real estate agent. The agent began by explain the housing market and what they could expect from the sale of the home.

"Sir, I know the house is in great shape and immaculate, but the school down the street has just been given a grade of "F" by the state. So, finding a young family with children or any family willing to buy here will be immensely difficult. You may need to consider asking substantially less and come down at least $40,000, or maybe more, if you want to sell."

Stan said nothing. He just dropped his head, walked slowly to the sink, and looked out of the window that Mary loved so much.

It was now time to say goodbye to the old house and have his daughter drive him back to her home. They stopped for a red light, and from the rear seat of the car he looked out. He could see after-school children laughing and horse-playing as they left Betty J's corner store, chewing their penny candy on their way home, full of hope and joy as his kids and their friends had done so often years ago.

The traffic light changed and they moved on, except for the image of the happy children of his neighborhood that he held in his mind. Stan slowly turned from the window and looked forward. He smiled. Nothing of real importance had really changed in his neighborhood.

Maybe someday someone would explain to him exactly what an "F" school was and why it meant that he now practically had to give his house away.

*It's 5:45 in the morning and still dark. Jack, a seven-year veteran, fully certified and licensed math teacher, is already awake. Lying in bed in his room at the Cross-Town Hotel, he is waiting for the phone to ring. The call will come soon advising him which school he needs to report to this morning. He no longer has a permanent school assignment.*

# No Place for Jack

~

THE PHONE RINGS AND HE answers, "Yes, this is Jack. Yes, I know where it is. You have a nice day too."

Struck out again. It's the notorious Jackson Middle School, not particularly kind to substitute teachers and a fifty-minute drive from his location, But, no time to lament—just dress, grab a quick cup of coffee, a donut, and hit the road.

As he approaches the interstate, it's clear that there must be an accident up ahead, for it looks like a parking lot as far as he can see. While waiting for traffic to move, he begins to reflect, how did this happen to me? Got my degree in math twelve years ago, banged around a few places, even taught overseas, and for the last seven years taught calculus and pre-calculus right here in this district.

Students in my last assignment voted me teacher of the year. So what did I do wrong? Why am I floating around the district without an assignment?

Moving again, Jack began to think about when things changed drastically. He knew that this district, like so many other urban school centers, had restructured their schools and replaced them with alternative schools like magnets and charters. But, could this explain why there were hundreds of surplus teachers without a specific assignment?

Then he thought about what happened right before school began. There must have been 300 of us there—all District Three teachers—all still unassigned: math, physics, English teachers, twenty-and thirty-year veterans, and much younger folks like me.

He remembered clearly what was said. "Ladies and Gentlemen: There are teaching vacancies in the district. Most of your former schools are now charters. Some are magnets. So, since you weren't kept by these schools, you will need to check the list of vacancies each morning on your computers, arrange for interviews, and secure one of the available vacancies."

Jack had followed these directions. He had 13—no—14 interviews and no fewer than 45 administrators had advised him by phone or during his personal visits to their buildings that the vacancies listed on the district's master list were inaccurate. "There are no math vacancies here, never were, or they were filled last week," he was told repeatedly.

Jack continued to ponder. Principals control their own budgets now. Do all the surplus teachers who were at the late August meeting simply cost too much? Could it be that simple, that calculated? The meeting I attended was for teachers in District Three.

There are four other districts, and each of them had a similar meeting. Are we looking at nearly 2,000 displaced, licensed, viable teachers? Is this phenomenon only occurring here, or is it also happening in other huge school systems like New York, San Francisco, Philadelphia, and Miami Dade County?

Jack finally arrives at today's assigned school. I hope I get a classroom assignment today, preferably in math. Last week four of my five days I had no classroom assignment. So I usually stayed in the teachers' lounge, except for last Wednesday when I volunteered to help the custodian move books.

After school, Jack went to the central office personnel department again just to check on his file. He was told, "No, Jack, there's nothing negative in your personnel file. As a matter of fact, there isn't much in your file at all."

Jack left the office more confused and discouraged than ever. Maybe, he thought to himself, I just need to get out of teaching.

That spring he reluctantly did. As he drove away, his Starbucks coffee spilled on his framed teacher of the year award lying on the passenger front seat. He watched as the coffee seeped under the glass. He wondered why he didn't try to stop it.

# ABOUT THE AUTHORS

**Raymond J Golarz** holds a BA degree in Sociology and a BS degree in Education from St. Joseph's College in Indiana. He received his master's degree and his Doctorate in Education from Indiana University. He taught middle school and high school and then served as the Director of Child Welfare Services where he supervised delinquency prevention and intervention programs and worked with the very poor and with delinquent gangs in the same neighborhoods where he spent his early childhood.

He taught psychology at St. Joseph's College, Purdue Calumet, Indiana University Northwest, and City College in Seattle. In addition, near Chicago he also taught Psychology for Law Enforcement for nearly ten years. He has been an assistant superintendent and superintendent of schools. He enjoys keynoting and has keynoted for school districts and major conferences in virtually every state in the United States and in most of the Canadian Provinces.

He is the co-author of *Restructuring Schools for Excellence through Teacher Empowerment*. He is the author of *Yellow Jacket Football In Hard Times and Good* and a companion book *When the Yellow Jackets Played*. These two books, using the backdrop of rugged American sandlot semi-pro football near Chicago, focus on the strengths of the early immigrants who came to America, and with their children lived the challenges of the Great Depression. With his wife Marion he Co-authored *On My Way Home I Bumped Into God, Sweet Land of Liberty, The Power of Participation* and *The Problem Isn't Teachers*.

All of his life, Ray has enjoyed sketching, oil painting, and woodworking. He and his wife Marion reside in Bloomington, Indiana.

**Marion Simpson Golarz,** the sixth of seven children, was born to Michael and Marion Simpson in 1940 in the quiet, Lake Erie town of Conneaut, Ohio.

Marion secured a BA in English Language Arts, and an MS in Education with a concentration in Reading. She taught English and remedial reading at the elementary and secondary levels as well as composition courses at Indiana University Northwest, Indiana University Southeast, and Purdue University Calumet where she also taught in the Writing Lab.

With her husband Raymond she has co-authored four books. *On My Way Home I Bumped into God, The Problem Isn't Teachers, Sweet land of Liberty and The Power of Participation.* They recently celebrated 50 years of marriage with their six children and their families, including 10 grandchildren.

Almost all of her personal writings began with thoughts written on the backs of napkins and scraps of paper. She has forever written poetry and prose. She reads virtually anything she can get her hands on, with her cat Patches sitting on her lap or her Boxer pup Cooper lying at her feet.

Ray and Marion can be reached at mjgolarz@live.com.

Printed in the United States
By Bookmasters